Technology, technology,
What have you done?
Given me the chance to show them
I am the one!

DO I HAVE TO BE A STARVING ARTIST IN THE 21ST CENTURY?

Hisani P. Dubose

4 Way Vision Productions Publishing
Bloomfield

Do I Have to be A Starving Artist in the 21st Century?

First Edition: March 19, 2010

Text Copyright © 2010 Hisani P. Dubose. All Rights Reserved.
Cover Layout and interior formatting by Dreaded Enterprises
Unlimited, Inc.
Original Illustration Copyright © 2009 Dadisi J. Dubose.
Produced by 4 Way Vision Productions, LLP

4 Way Vision Productions, LLP
147 Franklin St. Suite 208
Bloomfield, NJ 07003

ISBN-13: 978-1-451-55738-1
ISBN-10: 1-4515-5738-8
LCN: 2010900275

A 4 WAY VISION PRODUCTIONS PUBLISHING BOOK

Printed in the United States of America

10 9 8 7 6 5 4 3 2 1

Dedications

This book is dedicated to my mother, Dr. Johnnie M. Porter and my aunt, Mrs. Evelyn Taylor, LPN. My mother taught me to listen to my own voice and pursue it fearlessly. My aunt helped me learn the true meaning of family and the importance of supporting each other. I also dedicate this book to my son, Dadisi DuBose and daughter, Hakika DuBose, who grew up in the whirlwind of my life and still managed to become wonderful people.

To all the visual artists, dancers, musicians, cinematographers, directors, playwrights, screenwriters, novelists, set designers, production managers, game developers and designers, photographers, make-up artists, hair designers, stylists, costume designers, fashion designers, actors, singers, lighting designers, sound designers, and any types of artists I may have unintentionally excluded...this book is for you!

Special thanks to the Creative Arts and Technology Department at Bloomfield College - Bloomfield, NJ. I appreciate the opportunity to share information with eager students in such a comprehensive and innovative program.

An extra special thanks goes out to Dr. Tendai Ndoro and Denis Rasugu at the Rutgers Newark Small Business Development Center (SBDC). Dr. Ndoro and Mr. Rasugu helped me realize that I and all artists are entrepreneurs. They taught me how to develop a business plan made specifically for my industry. And finally, thanks to Steven Rosania who transferred the original cover artwork to digital format.

Table of Contents

Your Attention Please

The majority of my adult life I have been an artist, working onstage, backstage and both at the same time. I've also worked for two major arts organizations in New York and New Jersey. While working for Dance Theatre of Harlem (DTH) in the Publicity and Public Relations departments, I tried to absorb everything I could. I wanted to learn how to promote myself. This was a life changing experience and my introduction into the professional realm of the entertainment industry.

The greatest things I learned from watching Arthur Mitchell, the Founder of DTH, was to set high standards of professionalism, meet deadlines and to understand that you must develop an audience for your work. In the years since leaving DTH I have not met many people with the vision and drive of Mr. Mitchell. If you can imagine, here was a Black male ballet dancer who wanted to start a ballet company. At that time (in the sixties) there were few black ballet dancers and no black ballet companies.

Mr. Mitchell had to train dancers, find choreographers, raise money, get supportive staff (costume designers, technical people, etc.) and form a company. To understand the magnitude of this challenge, during that time the majority of African Americans had no interest in seeing ballet and White audiences didn't believe Black people could rise to the occasion because they had not seen it before. This meant that along with the challenge of starting a ballet company, he had to develop an audience for his work!

He methodically grew the company and their audience. Mr. Mitchell had the foresight to make the ballet school just as important as the company. To develop an audience Arthur use to invite the community and anyone else he could find, to the school for open houses. Attendees would see short performances and he would explain the goals of DTH. Not only did he form a ballet company, he developed an institution creating jobs for supportive staff.

I am sharing this information because no matter what your art, be it filmmaking, acting, screenwriting, dancing, game development, animation, visual arts, music, etc. you must be proactive in your career. You absolutely have to learn the business side of your field. If Arthur Mitchell had the dream of starting a ballet company and just started rehearsing dancers hoping to find somewhere to perform, Dance Theatre of Harlem would never have become an internationally acclaimed company.

He matched his artistic vision with a keen understanding of the business and worked incredibly hard. There are stories where people are "discovered" and success comes easy. All I can say to that is don't wait for it. It may happen for you that way but don't count on it.

The experience at DTH was an introduction for me. After leaving there, I was motivated to learn more about the entertainment business. Through trial and error, a lot of tears, reading and very lean times I have learned and learn more each day.

In high school I danced, played the flute and sang. I loved all three disciplines and could not decide which was more important to me. I was pretty good on the flute. Even got a few friends together and we formed a jazz group called Copper. We played a few local places (couldn't do clubs since we were not of legal age) and I thought I was a jazz musician. Then one day I heard Hubert Laws play the flute and realized I wasn't even close to being a professional.

In college I explored singing more and wound up performing with the college's gospel/jazz choir. We became the choir for a play called *Purlie*. It was such a good experience that three of us got together and decided to write a musical over the summer that could be performed at our college (Seton Hall University). I researched the play format and read a few plays. As it turned out, I was the only one who took the project seriously. By the end of the summer I had written the book and lyrics (and a few melodies) for my first play, *A Different Kinda Blues*. That was it for me! I realized that writing could utilize all my skills. I was also in the play. I eventually learned screenwriting because it gave my imagination more freedom.

My older brother Pepe has been telling me for years that I need to write a book to share what I've learned with other artists. The more I talk to artists of all ages and genres, the more I became convinced that he was right. I have spoken at a few universities, several film festivals, teach screenwriting and production as an adjunct at Bloomfield College in New Jersey and work on my own projects. I realize that most of us spend so much time learning and honing our craft that the business side can escape us.

There is a reason for this. If you are like me you probably hate that stuff. Who wants to be bothered negotiating deals, writing business plans, planning distribution strategies, etc. In my perfect world I would write screenplays, sell them and live a wonderful life. In the real world I had to learn production and how to direct. Being an independent filmmaker is a tough road to travel and you really need to know as much as possible if you want to earn a living. In the 21st century this is true of all genres.

The music business has changed drastically and continually. The old model of signing an artist, releasing a CD, producing a music video and live performances is filled with holes. People buy bootleg CD's, download music legally and illegally and the cost of everything has escalated. Labels are signing fewer artists and live shows generally make less money for the artists. As a result, recording artists now record their own music, release it on social networking sites and use a plethora of other avenues to sell their performances.

These types of challenges are faced by most professional artists. Part of the solution to finding a way in is to learn the business. If you are a singer, you can do local performances forever but will you ever make a living doing what you love? The same goes for other artists. You can be a master at your craft but how can you support yourself with your work?

I hope you will read this book and it helps you to realize that as an artist you are an entrepreneur. This will be explored more as we go on. Take control of your career!

Next in Line

There are different degrees of being an artist and all are good. Some people are talented at what they do (dancing, acting, filmmaking, visual, make-up, etc.) and decide it's best if they do what they love on a part-time basis. These are probably the sanest ones among us.

Then there are the driven artists who pursue their passion full-time and at some point realize they are not willing to pay the price required in terms of the struggle involved. Very few artists have an easy road to success. In this instance, success is defined as the ability to meet living expenses and live a somewhat comfortable life. In other words, being able to support yourself with your art.

The last group, to which I belong, are the artists whose art is a great part of their life's mission, their passion, their reason for breathing. People who are born to write, dance, paint, make movies, make music, etc. These artists can become tired of the constant struggle to make a living and swear off their work. They might even try another profession but they always come back because they have no choice. Sometimes they find a way to live in both worlds. Teaching and remaining a professional artist is one way to share your passion, hone your skills, make a living and still remain true to your life's mission.

Where does this passion come from? Is it passed on in families? That may be true. My father was a jazz musician who played with well-known big bands and singers of that era. My mother studied fashion design and was very talented in making beautiful outfits. She made the dresses and hats for my aunts wedding as well as dresses for my sister and I. Later in her life she took arts and crafts to a new level. Her house could have been on the cover of major home magazines. In her case art become a hobby and she wound up earning a doctorate degree in education.

Both my children are artists. My son an award winning illustrator and daughter an actress/choreographer/dancer who has appeared on two major TV shows. My younger brother Wolf got his BFA in Studio Art, went on to earn a Masters in Film & Television, won awards for filmmaking and has published two novels.

In my case perhaps it is a family thing, but I think all of us are born with certain abilities that we must cultivate. Anyone who has a passion for what they do professionally and pour themselves into their work is an artist no matter what their field. However, my focus for this book is on artists in the entertainment industry.

In this country (the U.S.) few people have time for you when you're up and coming. If you're asked, "What do you do?" and your answer is a writer, a dancer, a painter, a musician, a game developer, etc. more than likely the person questioning will look at you and say, "But what do you do for a living?" Or if you try to explain that your funds are low because you are in a slow period, you will be told, "You need to get a real job."

If you're an actor and you have a role in a movie or a filmmaker who wins awards at film festivals, those around you will get excited and want to identify with your "star power." When you don't do something spectacular within the next few months to a year, they get tired of waiting and figure its over for you.

In the entertainment industry, no matter what your art, be prepared to travel a lonely path. Most will not understand why you expose yourself to so much hardship. They don't understand that if there were an easy way out you would take it. There is nothing glamorous, sexy or exciting about struggling to pay rent, running out of food, or walking because you don't have bus or train fare.

My intent is to share information I've learned the hard way, hoping you will be spared some grief. It doesn't matter what age you are, if you went to school to study your craft or not. There are certain things that must be done if you are to survive your journey as a well-rounded person who can have a life outside of their work.

Michael Jackson was a brilliant, well-rounded artist. He was familiar with every aspect of his music and visual productions. His vision was incredible. I always believed he had total artistic freedom. Can you envision letting your imagination run without concerning yourself about money? He rode the upper levels of creativity into a different stratosphere. I've read on many occasions that he only felt alive on stage.

We all need an anchor to keep us grounded so we don't float away. Once in the creative zone, it is very easy to forget to eat, sleep, blow off important family functions, etc. This book is about understanding the entertainment industry, learning how to support yourself while honing your craft, understanding the artistic personality, and embracing the fact that as an artist you are also an entrepreneur.

First of All….

Before we go any further let's get something straight. Alcohol and drugs do not make your work better. I have heard this from so many people who say it does. It does not! All those people who tell you how deep, heavy and great the work is that you produce under the influence of whatever, they probably took some of what you had.

Many artists may turn to mind altering substances because they can't cope, are trying to escape some kind of pain or they're just physically exhausted. I'm sure the list of things that drive these actions are longer than this book will go into. But alchol and drugs do not make you better. There are always those who play at being an artist and think that the more messed up you get the more artistic you become. To these folks I say, grow up. We have lost far too many fantastically gifted people to legal or illegal abused substances.

Years ago I read in an issue of *Psychology Today* an article that explored the "Artistic Personality." The writer described how artists are euphoric when involved in their work and depressed when they are not able to work. The cycle has been documented. The writer suggested that what we have to do is learn how to handle the "in-between" times without loosing our minds. I never forgot that because it sounded as though the writer was a personal friend of mine who was sharing my secrets with the world. It made me feel that I was not crazy (well, maybe not totally).

It's amazing how little we know about ourselves and what makes us tick. Every time I share this information with fellow artists they are amazed. They wonder how I know this about them. I tell them to thank that writer whose name I don't remember.

A friend who is a brilliant animator/special effects whiz dropped out of sight for a while. A couple of years later he called and while talking mentioned that he had been so depressed they had him on medication. No one could figure out what was going on with him. He thought he was loosing his mind and went on to describe how he had not had any significant work in over a year. I began to laugh which of course disturbed him at first.

I explained what I knew about this "artistic personality" and how we all go through the euphoria/depression swing. My animator friend got quiet for a few seconds then asked how I dealt with it. I passed on some advice Danny Madden, a recording artist/producer friend once gave me. "When you have a slow spell, spend your time preparing." To that I add study your craft harder, read the trades, and stay mentally active in your profession. Stay on top of your game so you can come out fighting when the doors open again.

He was relieved and could not stop thanking me. This is something all of us must learn. Don't allow yourself to wallow in frustration and/or depression. Use the time wisely because when a break presents itself or you create one, you have to hit it hard!

I used to see Willie Cole, who is now a very successful visual artist, often in my travels. We would always compare notes;

"Your rent paid?"
"No my landlord is getting tired of my stories."
"Got any food?"
"No eating dirt again."
"Something's gonna' give soon."
"Yea, it needs to."
Then one day I was at the movies watching *Boomerang.* I always read the credits, it's the filmmaker in me. I had not seen Willie for a while. Suddenly I knew why.

When it came to the credits for the artwork, all of it was Willie's art. In the movie Hallie Berry's character was a visual artist so artwork was all over her house. I started yelling in the theater. How great was that?! Several months later I ran into Willie. I was so happy for him. He told me that for the longest time his house was full of his work. He could barely give it away. Then one day he hooked up with a gallery owner in Soho (NYC) and before he knew it everything was sold and now he was struggling to keep up with the demand.

The point is he utilized the slow time by producing. Please keep this in mind. It is really torture when money is low or non-existent and you can't seem to make or catch a break. Stay focused, keep working and don't listen to people who can cause you to feel bad about yourself. This is not to say that you should not work on making a living. We'll discuss that later. Just don't live in emotional limbo.

If you decide that you're tired and need to get out of the game, that's fine it's your choice. You don't owe anyone an explanation unless they've given you money. In that case you really must take the time to explain your actions to the benefactor or grantor. Otherwise, it's your life, do what works for you. Often we think a particular path is for us and we don't know its not until we travel in that direction for a while.

The Key Word is Industry

It always amazes me when I hear people in the performing arts go on about how they are the true artists. Somehow they believe that recording artists and filmmakers are compromised and are not really artists. To them I say, we all work in the entertainment industry which means the business side cannot be ignored.

As mentioned previously, I have worked with a few performing arts centers and organizations. The performance is about the art, but everything else is about business. Everyone is concerned with how many seats can be sold, what is the cost of the show, will it break even, etc. These are the same concerns of filmmakers and the recording industry. How many units will sell, will the theater sell out, was the project on budget?

None of us can get around the fact that entertainment is an incredibly big business. In the 21st century, if we want to work we must understand this. Unless you are independently wealthy and can do whatever you like without needing people to come see your performance or purchase your product, learn the business. It's an annoying necessity.

You may ask "why?" We spend so much time and energy expanding our art that having to deal with budgets, business plans and the other trappings of industry can be incredibly irritating. I used to feel sick and want to throw up whenever people started discussing these things. However, the world truly has changed. Realize that you are your product and whatever you produce is your product. In today's world you need to learn how to market and make money from your product. How to brand yourself.

Branding is important. It means that you or a product are identified with what you do by large numbers of people. Oprah Winfrey is a brand. The minute you say Oprah, everyone knows whom you're talking about, what she does and that her "brand" makes money. Pampers are such a big brand that when people need disposable diapers they say, "The baby needs some Pampers," even if they buy another brand. Branding yourself and your work gives you visibility and the ability to earn a living.

The music industry is in flux and it often seems the people who run it are not sure how it will be reconfigured. Between the Internet and bootlegged products, their sales have been hurt. How will the singer, jazz musician, classical musician, or any musician get a record deal? How will people hear your music? How will you get paid?

How will the filmmaker bring his/her projects to life? How can enough people see the work for it to make money? How can the actor break in? And how in the world will the writer or visual artist ever make a living? The truth of the matter is there is not a universal definitive answer to any of these questions.

There are things you need to do if you are serious about earning a living in your field. Two of these are listed below.

1. Learn your craft. Work hard and be the best you can. This means you must never stop learning and think you have arrived. When you stop learning you become stale.

2. Learn the business you are in! You may be the best at what you do. You may be drop dead gorgeous or handsome but the bottom line is people in the business look at you like a can of soup. They are interested in how much money they can make off of you. They are in business to make money and that's the bottom line.

How does understanding these two bits of information help you? Let's take the second one first. Since there is no universal principal regarding how you can break into the industry you have to be creative in developing opportunities for yourself. How can you do this?

Professional basketball players spend years developing their game. A player can develop the most beautiful 3-point shot in the world but if he can't sink it during a game, it's a great shot that never accumulates any points. This same player also needs other skills besides how to make that shot. He/she needs to be able to anticipate other player's moves, dribble and know all the complexities of the sport. You can be an outstanding painter, illustrator, screenwriter, director, singer, actor, game designer, but if you don't know how to put yourself in the game very few people will every be aware of your talent and you will not make a living doing what you love. So what's the solution?

- Study the industry!
- What are the trends?
- What's making money?
- Who are the players?

- What must you do to promote (brand) your work?
- Practice your pitch.
- Do research and be able to show how you will make money for the company.

Is this giving you a headache? I really do understand.
How can one study the industry?

1. Read the trade magazines and papers in your field! If you don't know what they are, find out. If you don't have the money to purchase them all go to the library. Yes you remember that place that has books. I say this because too many people believe everything can be done online. Some e-magazines sell online subscriptions which takes you back to a money problem. Call your local library and see if they carry the periodicals you need. If they don't, maybe you can form a network of like-minded people where all of you buy different magazines and pass them around.

2. Go to conferences, expos, festivals and other related events whenever possible. If you can't afford the admission fee, see if they need volunteers.

3. Get on email lists when you attend functions. You never know where you will find information.

4. While attending events and reading the trades, pay attention to trends and what's making money. Actor/Producer Will Smith said when he moved to L.A. he had his agent research the top selling genres in film. Once armed with that list, those were the only types of movies he considered. You don't have to do the same thing but it's an example of

how understanding trends can work for you. Does this mean you should change who you are and only run after trends? No, but if you understand the climate you can go after your dreams well armed.

5. Always carry business cards and ask the people you meet for theirs. This does not mean that if you run into George Lucas you shove a card in his hand and ask for his. He would more than likely throw it away. Can you imagine how many cards someone high profiled like him must receive? In that case, you would have to let him ask for your card.

6. Learn how to have short conversations and network. Number one rule- do not be phony or self-ingratiating. There are many ways to start a conversation without saying "what do you do?" Be creative. If someone is standing alone you may start out by saying, "I don't know anyone here do you?" Wait for an answer then introduce yourself and go from there. I'm not putting together a list of ice- breakers. There are other books for that or you can search the Internet. My point is be warm and real when starting conversations. Don't be afraid to talk. If you run into an important easily recognized person in your field, don't rush the person and try to be impressive. Sometimes its best not to approach the person if he/she is preoccupied. Pay attention to who is with him/her. Perhaps that person can be approached.

7. When there is someone you want to do business with go to the person's or company's website. Get

as much information as you can. Research helps you to become well informed.

8. Find out what types of contracts are used in your field. Read one. You cannot take the place of an attorney but you can have a working knowledge of legal standards. This will help you know what questions to ask when you do retain legal counsel.

9. Please, if you have the opportunity to speak with a major person in your industry and there is a line of people waiting to see the person, do not stand there talking for five minutes or more. If he or she is gracious enough to speak with strangers, don't hog the time and keep the line waiting. Say whatever you have to say in 60 seconds and move on. That is not the place to try and form a lasting relationship.

10. This is an ongoing process. Once you have a feel for the industry find out what information you need to have prepared to approach a person or company. Also, examine what you do and see how you can fit in, that is, how can they make money off of your skills? Here is a list of questions you need to consider. Some may not apply to your field so just use the ones that are relevant.

- Who is my audience?
- What is unique about me/my presentation/my work?
- How much money do I need to make my movie, record my music, create my new piece of art, etc.?
- What is my business plan?

- How can I improve my work?
- How are most people I know trying to get noticed?
- What different road can I take?
- What information should I have prepared in writing in case I meet someone I want to work with? Someone who could invest in my work or make an introduction for me.
- Do I have a website?
- What is my publicity/PR plan?
- Who can help with publicity/PR?
- What lawyer will I use?
- What does it take for me to attract a serious agent?

Here's a note on agents and managers. They make money directly from your ability to get paid for your work. Therefore, you have to plan to create a "buzz" about yourself. If your name is out there and you are making money, it will be easier to attract the agent or manager you need. Be very careful about signing any agreements. Make sure the person is legitimate. Definitely have an attorney read any agreements before you sign them. This is a rule of thumb. Otherwise you may find yourself tied to a situation that may take years to dissolve.

How can you check an agent or manager's credentials? Check their names on search engines, see if they are listed with your professional association (i.e. WGA, SAG, Actors Equity, Musician's union, etc.) and finally ask people in the industry.

Why does it benefit you to know who the players are in your industry? Back to my basketball analogy. If you are playing in a game and Shaquille O'Neal plays for the opposite team. Do you think it would help your game strategy by knowing who he is and how he plays? Of course it would. Even if the only thing you could figure out is be careful when trying to block him.

What if you were at a function and someone introduced you to the most important gallery owner in New York? If you are a visual artist and did not have a clue who this person was, what a missed opportunity! You could be standing next to the person who could change your life by just making a referral or telling you to call his office for an appointment. You don't have to go crazy trying to keep up with everyone in your industry but at least have a working knowledge of the players. Read the trades!

Another important thing to remember is to treat everyone well. Show everyone you meet respect and consideration. Do not become one of those people who searches out so called, "important people" and brushes everyone else aside. You should treat every person you meet as if they're important because they are. If you develop this approach to life you will go far. You never know whom you're talking to or standing next to. You can't snub a person because they aren't "important" then later find out who they are and take it back. Cover yourself by being good to everyone you meet.

Promoting yourself is essential. P.T. Barnum (Ringling Brothers Barnum and Bailey Circus) was known for attention grabbing promotional stunts. He was a master of shameless promotion. When he started his circus in the late

1800's, elephants, stilt walkers, all types of animals and performers in the circus would march through town to announce coming performances. Can you imagine the excitement that created? Do you think there was one person in that town who did not go to the circus? This was before television and the movies.

I'm not saying you should rent animals to march around with your name on them but you should have the same spirit. Be creative. If you send out press releases ask yourself why should anyone care about what you're doing. Too often because it's so important to us, we assume it is important to other people too. Well, it's not. Everyone is busy with his or her own life. If you want them to care about what you're doing you have to find a connection. Make what you're doing seem important to them.

A choreographer friend sent me an invitation to see her new work. It was a piece that explored the sound rocks make. During that particular time I was struggling to pay my rent, a potential investor had backed out of a deal without being considerate enough to let me know and a bunch of other maddening things were going on. Did I care at that time about the sound of rocks?

Give thought to who your potential audience may be then give them a reason to want to experience your work. As an exercise, think about the events you attended in the past six months. What made you get out of your house and go? Between cable TV and the Internet we can find a great deal of entertainment without walking out the door. I didn't even mention CD's, DVD's, DVR's and Blu-Ray. We have entertainment empires at our fingertips so what does it take to drag a person out the house to see or hear what you do? Again, pay attention, read, and watch entertainment magazine shows. Of course you can skip the ones that focus only on gossip.

If your form of entertainment goes into the home what makes yours stand out? Why should a person watch your show, your movie, listen to your music? Don't be afraid to talk to people who don't know you and ask them what they think about your work. In Manhattan on any given day you may see people stopping folks on the street asking them to come inside and watch a music video, a movie, a TV pilot at no charge. Then when the screening is over, they will pass out questionnaires to get feed back.

The Internet allows great opportunities to do market research (that's what this is called). You can upload music, artwork, a trailer, photographs, etc. and post the work on social networking sites, asking people to email you with their opinions. Or don't ask for opinions. Just send the information and see what type of responses come back. You can also send emails to a select list. Whatever you do in this direction just remember to keep it short. Advertisers have found that the average adult in the U.S. has an attention span of 30 seconds. Keep this in mind.

Understanding the short attention span of most adults is another reason why it's important to practice your pitch. When you run into someone who might be a good contact, as mentioned previously, you must be able to say your piece quickly. Practice making your case in 60 seconds without speed talking. If you plan ahead you can say who you are, what you do and what you're looking for in that time. You should really be able to say it in one sentence. Whatever you do, if money is what you need, do not ask for it in your 60-second pitch. All you need to do is pique interest in you and/or your project. The money conversation comes later, after the person has shown interest. If you want to kill the opportunity ask for money up front.

I was on a panel at a film festival in Philadelphia two years ago. We were focusing on screenwriting. My co-panelist listened to me discuss the importance of knowing the business after we talked about developing strong stories. Once the event was finished he asked if putting emphasis on the business interferes with my abilities as an artist. I told him that understanding the business has made it possible for me to work as an artist.

Years ago I did feel conflicted. Wondering if being and artist/entrepreneur would contaminate my work and pull my energies in opposite directions. As I pondered this eternal question I had made very little headway as an artist. Getting tired of not having enough food, money, recognition, etc. I realized that I'd better do something. So, I started paying attention to the business.

Our brains can handle a lot more than we ask of them. You can do both. You have to. At some point you will be able to turn more of the business over to agents and managers. You will be very well informed after having done the work yourself and possess the ability to articulate intelligently exactly what you want. Your chances of being ripped off will be reduced because you will know the business.

Knowing the business changes your whole conversation. If you are an independent filmmaker, when talking to potential investors you will show how your talent is giving them the opportunity to make money. Most of us start out with the attitude that we are asking them to do us a favor by investing. It's totally different when you can show them how to make money with you. The same is true for any genre.

You are an entrepreneur and your art is your business! This understanding will take you further than the "please help me" stance. This is not to say that you should be arrogant. No. Just be confident. Knowing what you're talking about gives you confidence. Just make sure you also stay on top of your artistic game.

How Can I Support Myself: The Big Question!

No matter how great we are at what we do there are realities we all must face; food, clothing and shelter. We cannot escape these vital, nagging necessities. The starving artist seems to be a romantic concept in the movies but there is nothing glamorous about being hungry. Even if you have a spouse, parent, other half, benefactor, etc. who supports you, eventually you have to bring in some cash. Yet no matter how hard we try to project a time line, you really have no idea when the doors will open and you will be able to consistently support yourself with your art.

I have met many people who were very good at their art but let it go because they could not handle the financial roller coaster. An acquaintance who is a screenwriter and author of several successful books works full-time in the corporate division of a major cable network. He admonishes writers to leave the profession. Do anything but suffer the pain and poverty that can come with being a writer. He is so emphatic that on several occasions I've heard him speak at film festivals where he revealed that if his children ever said they wanted to be any kind of artist, he would lock them in their rooms until they agreed to become part of a more stable profession. He may have been kidding about locking the kids up, but the sentiment was dead-on serious.

A woman I know was one of the producers of an academy award-winning movie. She called being a producer a "miserable life." With several successes under her belt she still had to fight hard to get financing for new projects. She had finally worked out a deal with a major cable network and thought she could breathe again. Then the World Trade Center was attacked. Not only was the country paralyzed, so was the entertainment industry. This woman's deal was killed, never to be resurrected. The last time I spoke to her she was giving up her apartment and moving in with family. The next time I reached out, her phone was disconnected.

So, how can artists avoid the Feast or Famine Syndrome? For years, every time I met any kind of artist I would always ask, "how do you support yourself?" I was always hoping to hear something that would give me a solution. The truth is, if you put all your time into a full-time job your life's work becomes part-time and your full potential may not be reached. This is not to say you should never take a full-time gig. I hate to sound contradictory, but as I mentioned before there is no one solution for everyone.

Here's what I have learned that may help you. The minute you realize that you are an artist who must pursue your passion, start planning. What will you plan? You should explore opportunities to create residual income. What is residual income? We all understand residual income in the form of royalty payments but there are other forms. Residual and Passive income are principles that can stabilize your life, lead to wealth, control of your time, and a way to break the cycle of struggling.

Residual income requires that you put in the work to develop income that will be paid to you continuously. Eventually this income becomes passive, meaning that once the work is done, after a while the money comes without much further work being done. Examples of this type of income are real estate investments, books, music, movie or patent royalties, online advertising revenue, online affiliate programs, network marketing, click-through income, etc. Research these subjects. You may find one or more that can produce income for you.

I read an article about Arnold Schwarzenegger several years ago. It said that when he came to the U.S. he purchased some income producing real estate which meant he always had an income. This allowed him to focus full-time on his acting and bodybuilding pursuits without worrying about supporting himself. This was an eye opener for me. What brilliance! Wish I had thought of it! However, by the time I read this I had already been riding the income roller coaster. There was no money to purchase real estate. If I had understood the importance of residual income when I started out, my life would have been less stressful. There would still be a certain amount of struggle but it would not have been for the basics. My full attention would have been on advancing as a professional.

No matter where you are in your career, it's important that you seriously rethink how you earn money. So many people advise artists to develop something to "fall back on." That expression has always bothered me because it implies you will fall or fail. Instead I say develop at least two or three income streams. Take the time to explore avenues of potential residual income that fit who you are and how you work.

Think like a wealthy person instead of a struggling artist. Donald Trump has been quoted as saying network marketing is a viable way for someone who was not born wealthy to acquire wealth. Consider it. I got involved in a network marketing company in the health and wellness industry. When I started approaching people I knew they said, "I thought you were a filmmaker. Why are you doing this?" At first I felt kind of bad because they were really wondering if I had given up on my life's work. I thought for a few days then my answer was, " I'm using this as another vehicle to raise money for my projects."

Always examine your abilities and find a way to earn money on your own terms. What skills do you have that can earn money based on your schedule? Are you bilingual or multilingual? An entrepreneur I know from Haiti speaks three languages so he worked his way into being an interpreter for the court in his town.

Another friend, Leslie Ford, who is a brilliant Jazz musician took a correspondence course and became a locksmith. If you change your way of thinking, any little skill you have can turn into a side business. One day I began speaking with a lady sitting next to me in the library. She noticed I looked troubled and asked if I was all right. I explained that I needed a legal way to make more money without it interfering with the time I needed to work in my career. She told me to make three lists when I got home but to relax before I started. On one list I would write down everything I was good at, all my skills. The other would include everything I've done (work experience) and the last list encompassed everything I wanted to do.

This sounded overly simple but I went home and followed her directions. I was surprised at how long each list became. Once the lists were completed I realized I was looking at my life, objectively, for the first time. This process clarified a lot for me. At that time I was working with and an older Jazz vocalist, helping him run his production company. I had been performing as a vocalist and writing movies on the side.

I figured if I could get a recording contract it would place me in a position to get my movies made. I had been singing and writing my own material professionally for a while and this vocalist who was signed with Warner Brothers promised to hook me up with his Warner contacts to get me signed.

Working with this company really helped me to see that until you prove you can sell millions of records you have little control over your career. This was in the early nineties when record labels still ruled the music world. At that point in my life, I had too much experience to act mindless and be led around by people who were always looking for the next big thing. I asked several A&R people what they were looking for. Their answers were amusing, "The next Janet Jackson," "I'll know it when I see it," "The next Prince," etc.

Give me a break! So after examining my lists, I realized I should be running my own production company instead of someone else's. My screenwriting mentor once told me I would discover that I had to produce my own work because my vision was different from the normal standard of things. He said people might not understand until they see my work. I did not want to believe him at the time. All this was hard enough now I have to produce too? Ahhhh!

The lists made me realize that my experience with music, dance and writing dictated that I should have a company and use it to write and produce my own work. I felt a clarity that relaxed me. Looking at the lists I saw that I had the skills and experience. One of my side gigs had always been writing proposals for small non-profits. Ninety-five percent of the time they got funded. I had helped these organizations raise millions dollars cumulatively so why couldn't I do the same for my company?

I formed my company and began calling myself an independent filmmaker. This immediately sent me on a course to learn more about my newly defined craft. The late Claude Brown, author of *Manchild in the Promised Land* and I went to the same gym. When I told him I needed to master the screenwriting format he directed me to the Syd Field book on screenwriting. Told me it was the bible of the field.

I bought the book and inhaled it. Then I found out about a course the Writer's Guild of America, East was sponsoring with the Writer's Voice in New York. It was a nine-week intensive screenwriting course that would only accept twelve people and cost more than I could afford. To be considered, a full script had to be submitted.

Armed with my Syd Field book, I hammered out a screenplay and was accepted. I worked in the office of the Writer's Voice to pay off the tuition. There are many steps I've taken between then and now but it all started with the lists I made. I don't care where you are in your career make the lists.

No matter what your discipline, you should form a company. The quickest and cheapest way is to form a Sole Proprietorship. You can register with your county, get a tax I.D. number from the IRS and you're in business for less than $100. The advantage of this is any money you make goes to your company. Then you pay yourself and take care of your expenses. You will be able to deduct every expense related to your work including meetings, materials, clothing, travel, in some instances make-up, hair care, etc.

Having a company and being an entrepreneur definitely helps you to keep more of the money you make because you have more deductions. Try to keep yourself straight with the IRS. You don't want them coming after you once you finally begin to make serious money. There is one thing you should know about having a Sole Proprietorship. After five years if you don't show a profit, they will disallow your deductions and call your business a hobby. It's in their books that if a Sole Proprietorship is not profitable in five years, it is not a business.

I know because this happened to me and I'm still paying off my bill from a previous year. If you have a corporation, this will not be a problem. Consult an accountant about the best type of corporation for your needs.

In summary, the best way to support yourself until your profession can support you is to:

1. Develop a plan to make residual income and follow it.
2. Make the 3 lists of all your skills, experience and what you want to do.
3. Seriously think about what your lists say about you.
4. Use your talents to make legal money.

5. Change your way of thinking. Think like a wealthy person, not a struggling artist.
6. Never stop learning. Read books about successful people no matter what their business. This will help you to keep in mind that when you travel off the beaten path, its not easy but you can reach your goals.
7. Be fearless!
8. If you have to work a full-time job learn everything you can while there. You never know what learned skills may be needed in artistic work
9. Let your work ethic remain in the realm of excellence even if it's your day job. You never know whose watching. Besides your standards should remain high no matter what you're doing.

Up and Coming With Children

The ideal situation is to wait until you have a certain amount of success in your career before having children. This is logical. However, when it comes to us humans, logic and plans do not always prevail. So what happens when you already have children before you discover your life's work or they pop up along the way?

If you're a male, your wife or the baby's mother will probably be responsible for the day-to-day care of the children. There are exceptions of course, but I'm speaking generally. Female artists who are mothers have more to deal with. Several I know rely on mothers or other family members to help with children. The man in their life may be working and cannot offer much help until after work.

The single female parents are another story still. What happens if you don't have family support? Many families like mine are scattered around the country. What can you do for babysitters? I was a single parent through divorce. My son and daughter are ten years apart so it was almost like I had two "only" children.

This gave me the flexibility to take them everywhere I went. Well almost everywhere. Both have been on stage with me, backstage, at meetings, in classes, everywhere. Of course this meant I had to plan how I worked. Whether performing or writing I produced most of my work. This way I could bring a child with me. If other people hire you no matter how well your children behave they don't want them around.

So I never stopped working in my profession. I just could not always move as fast as I wanted. I promised myself and God that my children would not suffer because of my work. So between making survival money, pursuing my career and raising my son and daughter, I didn't have much time for a social life. However, since everything I did involved meeting and speaking with other people, I never felt like I was missing anything. There were always folks around me.

If you are on this journey with children, put them first! They deserve it and if you don't put them first in your life, who will? It's definitely not easy and requires a tremendous amount of patience, determination, love, flexibility, endurance, creativity and faith. We must remember these are human beings and how we act impacts on every aspect of their lives. Again, it's not easy.

An outstanding Jazz musician I know worked hard taking care of his family and at his art. His schedule would include getting up at 5:00 AM to practice his trumpet for an hour, and then he went to work as a locksmith at a university for eight hours. After work there would be rehearsals and time with the children. Most of his gigs would be after work and weekends.

He told me that sometimes after performances where he was in the zone, being one with the music, the drive to work the next day was unbearable. He would force himself into the building to make sure his children could be fed. He eventually softened this dilemma by founding the Jazz Institute of New Jersey. This non-profit Institute made it possible for him to work in music everyday while teaching children the ins and outs of jazz. The Institute also taught its students life skills with the music.

He still worked at the university but got them involved on a small scale. This took some of his frustration out of going to work because it now helped serve his artistic purpose. Leslie continued to play and eventually moved into playing corporate gigs since they paid more and he didn't have to stay out all night.

His story is important because it's an example of putting your children first and finding a way to feed your passion. The Jazz Institute of New Jersey is now twenty years old, they have trained over nine hundred students and Leslie is still on top of his music game.

It is important that you enjoy your kids and not view them as an obstacle to your success. Helping a child grow up is a laboratory for creativity. Children can teach you the depth of love. Who is more creative than a child? Just watch how a child plays. People have often asked me if I regretted having my son and daughter. My answer is no. They have opened up feelings and understanding that I'm sure I would not have been able to tap other wise. Children can open up new layers of depth in anyone but especially artists.

So if you don't have children yet should you run out and get some to become a better artist? Of course not. It's a tough road to travel even though rewarding. This chapter has been written to offer support if you already have a family or if one pops up.

I mentioned that my father is a Jazz musician. Once he found out that my mother was carrying me he took a full-time job at a supermarket and played nights and weekends. I grew up around constant music. When he played local shows with well-known performers my sister and I often got to watch from backstage. We also attended the local gigs at parks and schools.

I used to love it when he would come home late at night from playing and bring home Chinese food. My mother would get angry when he woke us up to eat but we had fun. My parents were divorced when I was nine. It was an incredibly painful time for us all. I remember the music that was on the radio during that time. When I hear those songs I still remember the sadness. Eventually my father remarried. His new wife was not a secure person and did not want him to travel outside of her domain so eventually he became isolated from his musical world. I don't know if he slowed down because he was tired of the grind or to please her, but the point is we all make decisions.

Your children may never become artists but include them in what you do. Let them get to know your world. No matter what road they choose, they will be empowered by understanding and experiencing your world. You will be surprised at what they learn. My son, who has been drawing everyday since he got old enough to hold a crayon, was always a little shy in front of people he didn't know.

I was preparing to go to a meeting one day when he was five. I watched him scoop up a bunch of his pictures and put them in his book bag. When I asked what he was doing, he announced that he was an artist and would sell his pictures at my meeting. I thought that was cute and said okay. So off we go. At the end of the meeting he quietly asked if he could sell his pictures now. I laughed and said sure.

My "shy" son stood up and announced that he was an artist and he was selling his pictures for one dollar each.

Everyone thought it was cute until he went around the room showing his work asking which one they wanted. The boy left there with twenty dollars. I was shocked. From then on, all during his life he sold his pictures to raise money for camp, comics, etc. He now has a degree in animation but loves illustration so he decided to try teaching because he wants to help urban youths. He sees art as a vehicle to learn about life.

My daughter grew up around her brother's constant drawing. She also is a talented visual artist and had it as her major in high school. However, by her second year she had enough. Drawing was fun to her but not when she had to do it everyday.

She had taken dance classes off and on during her life but did not seem to be interested in pursing dance. While attending a summer art and music camp for two summers before she started high school, dance touched her heart.

Once back home she searched for a dance school where we lived. We used to pass Sharon Miller's Academy of the Performing Arts on a regular basis since it was in the middle of a major thoroughfare. My daughter mentioned casually that she might be interested in taking classes there. Sharon Miller was a former principal dancer with the Alvin Ailey American Dance Theater.

One day my daughter came home with information about the cost and the schedule and asked if she could start classes. The next thing I knew she decided to become a dancer. Instructors at the school loved her passion and pushed her to be her best. From there she got a B.F.A. degree in Modern Dance. Since then she has been acting and dancing. She was one of the dancers chosen to audition for Michael Jackson's tour just before he passed away. She could not believe while watching his memorial service that thirty days before then she was auditioning for him on that same stage.

I never tried to influence my children to become artists. I used to jokingly say I never meant to pass on the curse. Well maybe I was half joking because I didn't want them to travel such a difficult road. What I did do was support whatever they were interested in. It's important to encourage your children to explore their interests. Children who have passion about something don't usually get in trouble. Their minds are filled with their dreams. We have to provide a way for them to become involved in their passion. It will probably change many times but they must explore.

In conclusion, you can be an artist with children. You just have to work hard, put them first and keep them safe. Spoil them with affection but make sure they learn manners, discipline and that other people are important. A well-behaved child can go with you anywhere but nobody wants to be around "BeBe's Kids". If you don't know this reference, let me put it another way, brats scare people away so don't turn your children into little monsters by not teaching them anything or making them think the world revolves around them

It's really important to give your child some type of spiritual training. They, like us, have to know that there is an entity greater than us who loves them. You won't always be with them. They need a conscience and a shelter. This is also important for you.

Also, eliminate things and events you don't need in your life. This will create more free time and space for your career and kids. For example, if you have friends who always lean on you and wind up taking up a lot of your time, let them go. You can't raise adults but you must raise your children. You can still love these people but stop letting them take up your time.

Make sure that no matter what you are doing, they unquestionable know that you love them and will be there when they need you!

How Will You Weather the Storms?

I am probably one of the few people in the world who does not welcome the coming of summer. Not because I don't love the weather but because in the past it was a hard time to make money. I'm an adjunct instructor at Bloomfield College (NJ). This has helped to keep me afloat during the year and it leaves time for me to focus on my writing and raising money for productions

I have worked a few full-time jobs. One at an arts center. This kept the money consistent but I was putting in twelve and fourteen hour days 60% of the time. I would plan my schedule so that during my vacation time I would shoot a movie. Between working those hours, writing and pre-production I was working two full-time jobs. I also had to take care of my daughter because by then my son was on his own.

I worked at that art center for six long years. I started as a consultant then became full-time. By then the politics of it all and the hours were taking a toll. I had developed a potentially serious health problem and didn't even know it. I had the scourge that few speak of publicly but women, especially African Americans, are plagued by the big F, fibroids.

I knew I had uterine fibroids but the doctor said as long as they didn't interfere with my quality of life we'd leave them alone. For those who don't know what they are, they are non-cancerous growths that develop inside the uterus. Depending on their location they can cause a lot of pain or just cause incredibly heavy bleeding during menstruation.

Fibroids take years to grow and eventually will cause problems.

I was always feeling tired and on occasion light headed. I attributed it all to working so many hours. Had I not been pulling the long days and nights, I would have figured out that I was anemic. By the time I accidentally discovered how severely anemic I was, the doctor told me it was time for the little buggers to be removed.

My anemia had been so severe that it took eight weeks for me to get back to normal after the surgery. I stayed at the job for one more year then left. I reasoned that if I was going to be working so hard and long it should be for me. Two months before I quit, I started the New Jersey Movie Maker's Network.

The Network was a service organization for New Jersey's independent film community and anyone who worked in or provided services for us. We held monthly workshops to provide information to help move people's projects forward and charged a small fee to join. Non-members were welcomed at events they just didn't get the member discount. The response to the Network was great. We had no idea there were so many people in New Jersey making movies and working in the field. I had planned for this to be my day job. I would be surrounded by filmmaking on all levels and be able to pay my living expenses. I was surprised at how many industry people in New York and New Jersey came out to facilitate our workshops.

We had many behind the scenes stars like Monty Ross who co-produced most of Spike Lee's early work, Bill Mesce from HBO Corporate, Michael B. Jordan (actor from The Wire, The Sopranos, etc), Shelley Palmer (Director of New Media for the Academy of Television Arts and Sciences- you know, the people who give out the Emmy Awards), Marc Jacobson (Entertainment Attorney with Greenburg Traurig, a law firm with one of the largest entertainment divisions in the country), Dwayne Hunter Ferguson (former Art Director for Marvel Entertainment), the list goes on.

The amazing thing about operating NJ Movie Maker's Network was the personal benefit I received. I learned a tremendous amount, we were able to really help get information out to students, professionals, novices and people began working together on projects. JVC of America, Professional Products Division did outstanding workshops for us every year. Their District Sales Manager at the time, Diana Janos, would introduce new cameras and equipment each year. She even brought in the engineer who designed one of the cameras.

We made such an impact within the state that smaller organizations like ours began to pop up all over the place. Eventually we were invited to produce a film festival at Bloomfield College. I was reluctant at first because that is another kind of business. We were about information and connecting. However, I could not pass up the opportunity to use the space. The Westminster Arts Center at the college became our partner in producing the festivals and the workshops which meant we no longer had to pay to use space.

For five years we did great work and inspired a lot of filmmakers. The problem was that the venture began to lose money. We never became a non-profit because the major philanthropies in the state said they could not support the work we were doing. If the foundations in your home state don't support your work, it's almost impossible to get money from others. We would have been a non-profit, stuck with the paperwork required of such organizations, with no money coming in.

Our money came from membership fees, events and small sponsorships. The other problem was, since I am a filmmaker I could not devote 100% of my time to continue building and funding the organization. The other two wonderful women who helped run the Network, Carol Spann and Henrietta Parker, also had full-time pursuits and could not be there full-time.

So after five years we put the Network to rest and we were all better for the experience. Financially, I was a mess. I had used my meager funds to fill in the gaps of the network for the last two years. During this time both my children were in college and I had a house. In the middle of all this mayhem, I managed to produce a documentary with no money called, *The Vanishing Black Male.*

We got Melvin Jackson, Jr. who had just appeared in a season of the HBO series, *The Wire*, to be the interviewer. I wanted a young African American male who looked like part of the hip-hop generation to ask the questions. So Lloyd (the cameraman who had an old DV camera), Carol, Melvin and I set out on a grueling two-day schedule to interview twenty-seven people.

I set up the interview schedule beforehand, sent Melvin a train ticket to come from Maryland, got my son to develop original artwork to be used in transitions and off we went. Most of the people interviewed were African

American men from various walks of life. We got some outstanding interviews. Now the dilemma was post-production money.

A friend of mine, Theresa, had just sold her house and I thought she said she would invest $2,500.00 for post-production. In the meantime, I made up brochures designed to solicit $40.00 donations from anyone who stood still long enough to listen. The idea was, if they gave us $40.00 toward post-production costs, we would list them and their business if they had one, in the credits and invite them to the premiere. I went to every networking event I could find armed with my brochures. In a month I raised about $800.00 this way.

In the meantime the money came through and the checks cleared from the sale of Theresa's house. She called and said she would pick me up to go pick up the checks from the attorney's office. When she came out of the office she was explaining that my bank might hold the check for a while since it was a big check. You know all that business with the Patriot Act since 9/11 made banks take longer to clear checks....

Anyway, she handed me the check and I was speechless. I thought she said $2,500 but she said $25,000.00. When I finally started breathing again, she laughed and could not understand how I misunderstood what she said. That was such a blessing.

We could never have completed post-production on the money I raised. Al Santana who is an outstanding filmmaker in his own right has an editing studio in Brooklyn. We worked many hours putting together the footage. There were several problems as always with productions. Since we interviewed people in their surroundings and relied on natural lighting, there were lighting issues that took time to correct.

There were sound issues. The interviews took place in the summer, a very hot summer and many of the air conditioners were noisy. We had to choose between interviewees dripping with sweat or background noise. We wound up going to Harvest Works in Manhattan to correct the sound problems.

There was a problem with the format the cameraman used. This led to us having to get the DV tapes transferred to DVCAM at Rafik Studios in New York before we could even play the footage on Al's system. Anyway, as usual, our no money production cost money in post-production. Thanks to our Executive Producer, Theresa we were able to pull it off.

I secured an Internet distributor while attending the IFP (Independent Feature Project) convention in Manhattan. I went there carrying a few copies of our documentary with the intent of speaking to the cable network people who were presenting about picking up *The Vanishing Black Male*. They smiled and acted interested but of course nothing ever happened.

I visited all the vendors. There was a woman from a distributor called Indiepix. We talked and she explained how they operated. I liked the fact that the company was run by someone with a history in various aspects of the entertainment the business. Indiepix offered DVD on demand which meant a small start-up cost for our distribution. At that time the company was less than a year old. They were hungry.

The following week Theresa and I went and met with the owner of the company, Bob Alexander. We agreed on everything. It was very important to me to have distribution in place by the time the documentary premiered which by the way would take place in 30 days. Bob rose to the occasion. I gave him a DVD master, the artwork and we were up and running on their website by the premiere.

Since this book is for all artists I won't get too deep into distribution but I will say this. No matter what your art, you have to deal with distribution in some form. Study your options and don't always shoot for the big guys. If you are building your brand (you are your brand) understand that the big guys may take you on but the ones bringing in the most money the fastest get top priority. You need a distributor who will work with you to build your brand and sales. You also want to get paid in a reasonable manner. The big guys have a maze of accounting systems that can be difficult to follow unless you can hire an auditor who plays on their level. So in the beginning be very careful and thoughtful.

So back to the story, *The Vanishing Black Male* opened at the Robert Van Fossan Theater, presented by NJ Movie Maker's Network (See how helping others paid off. I got to premiere my own movie without my name being anywhere except in the credits.). Flyers were available to let the audience know where to purchase the movie. It all came together on time and we got many orders that night.

Remember, I was doing all this in the middle of a personal economic mess. When I developed the budget for the money Theresa invested, I was able to include a small salary for myself for the three months leading up to the premiere. I set the premiere date before we went into post-production. This gave us a time-line to work with. The salary made it possible for me to devote 100% of my attention to the project.

This did not change the fact that my house was about to go into foreclosure. So after the movie premiered and was received very well I still was in a very stressful personal situation. We had sent a press release out via BlackPR.com, a fabulous press release service that went to every major black-based newspaper, radio station, magazine and television network around the country. Thank God we had money to do this because it really helped put us on the map.

I noticed that a movie critic's reviews were on their site on a regular basis. I contacted the site's representative and asked what we had to do to be reviewed by this critic, Kam Williams. The owner of the company, Dante, sent the critic's email address. I emailed Mr. Williams and asked how I could get *The Vanishing Black Male* reviewed. He answered and explained that it was the end of the year and he had a stack of movies to review but to send it to him and if he could get to it he would. I sent him a DVD and forgot about it since he didn't sound like it would happen.

Earlier in the year I had entered one of my screenplays, "Nobody Will Know" in Producer/Director Francis Ford Coppola's American Zoetrope Screen Writing Competition and never heard from them.

I had contacted Mr. Williams in October. I was sitting at my computer in December, wondering how I could keep my house and just feeling really down. The DVD was selling but very slowly. I had been doing everything I could think of to promote the movie. I had to make a $1,000.00 payment to my daughter's college so she could register for the next semester, I had been eating peanut butter and jelly sandwiches for two weeks and a few eggs here and there...you get the picture.

Then as always, when it looks impossible I find something to laugh at. If the people in the NJ Movie Maker's Network and those who attended my movie's premiere could see me now, what would they think? I thought the irony was hilarious. I checked my email and was surprised to find Mr. Williams had written. So I quickly opened his message and had to read it three times to be sure I read it correctly.

I had no idea that Kam Williams was a syndicated movie critic. He sent a copy of his latest syndicated article that listed the best and worst movies of the year, the best directors and actors. In the documentary category, he called *The Vanishing Black Male* the best Black documentary of 2005. Then under Directors, he called me the Best Black Director of 2005.

He had Thomas Carter, a director whose work I love, listed as number two, under me. I must have sat there quiet for about fifteen minutes. After all, I had been living on peanut butter and jelly on whole wheat for two weeks. Perhaps I was hallucinating. Then I finally jumped up and started yelling. I cannot explain what I felt.

The money situation had not changed but at least my work had been recognized. Once I finished jumping around and screaming I did face reality. Even though I was listed above Thomas Carter, a man who had been directing major motion pictures for years and some of my favorite TV shows, I understood that I still had a lot to learn and this did not mean I was a better director than Mr. Carter. It's important to keep things in perspective.

I have seen a lot of filmmakers win awards and receive recognition who thought they had arrived. Suddenly you could barely talk to these people. I see it this way, if George Lucas whose work has changed the industry, is still learning and growing, have I arrived? This wonderful accolade inspired me to do better.

I did a Google search on my name to discover that Mr. Williams' article had gone to so many publications that I now had several pages under my name search. I also discovered something else. I had placed as a quarter finalist in the Frances Ford Coppola Screen Writing Competition! Could my heart stand this? I was tempted to call my mortgage company and say, "Do you know who I am?" That thought really made me laugh because they would have said, "Okay so where's the money."

Eventually my house was sold in a quick sale to keep from being foreclosed. The timing was perfect because I was able to pay my daughter's college and had some money left to travel to film festivals where our movie was being screened. I had been there a little less than eight years so there was not a lot of equity in the house but at least the bank got paid off. Had I understood more about general business at that point I would have invested in some type of mutual fund. Even if it was only a few hundred dollars.

One problem most artists have is that we spend so much time trying to get where we need to be that we don't plan enough. By the time we get a lump sum of money it usually goes to pay our back bills and if we aren't careful we're broke again in a few weeks. I saw in an interview that recording artist Lionel Richie said it was not until the success of his second platinum album that he actually felt like he had any money. Money from the first went to pay everyone he had owed for years.

I remember the late-great comedian Richard Pryor said in an interview after having tax problems that when he started making serious money, he spent it. He had been struggling so long that he bought the things he wanted. His accountant at the time had to sit him down and explain that he had to form a production company and put himself on the payroll with a steady salary. He could not just spend half a million dollars without paying Uncle Sam.

I have learned that this is the right approach whether you make a thousand dollars or several billion. Always include a salary for yourself in the budget and keep track of your money. Even when you can afford an accountant, be aware of where your money is going.

Several years ago Bill Cosby talked about how he got ripped off during the early years of his career. His advice was to always sign your own checks. This keeps you aware of how your money is spent. Otherwise you won't have a clue. We must consider these things and have a plan for our money before we make it. Why? Because its feast or famine. Either money is scarce or when it does come it comes quickly. Be prepared for it to come so you won't be overwhelmed.

To weather the turbulent storm of the entertainment industry you need several things in place and lots of prayers. Here are a few items to consider:

- Take some quiet time to think about who you are and what you stand for. Develop a clear picture and define yourself. Do not let other people define you or you will loose your mind. He's too tall, not tall enough, too fat, too skinny, not talented, a genius, etc. Even though we all grow and change you must have a solid understanding of you. There is a saying, "If you don't stand for something you'll fall for anything."
- Keep a few people around who understand what you're doing and who will tell you the truth. Do not surround yourself with folks who always agree with you. Truth helps you grow. Lies lead to stagnation!
- Understand that there will be family members and others who love you and are afraid for you. They don't want to see you suffer and struggle. So when they urge you to do something else or think you're not dealing with reality, remember it's coming from love and fear. Take it easy on them and don't allow their fear to wreak you. Don't you become afraid.
- As mentioned previously, when the money and opportunities are slow, spend the time preparing yourself. Do what you can to make legitimate money and do what it takes to be on top of your artistic game.
- Again, it's never too late to find sources of residual income. Even if you have to deal with a network marketing opportunity, real estate, an Internet affiliate program, etc. It's worth the investment of time and some money if it means you will have a

steady cash flow. You may not get rich but if it pays the rent/mortgage and feeds you, why not?

- Keep a food survival box. Do this based on your tastes but here are some suggestions; Dried beans, rice, peanut butter and jelly, crackers, whole grain bread, dried fruit, nuts...you get the idea. You have to keep food around so if you hit a dry spell you won't starve. Also, when you have money, feed your hungry friends when you can. Its true that what goes around comes around.

- Develop a spiritual base. If you have not experienced this yet, there will be times when you doubt yourself, feel alone and question your own sanity. You need to have a higher power you believe in and can talk to. You have to have faith to get through the hard times. There are things you will tell God that you would never share with anyone else.

- Once you get over any crisis in confidence, remember the success and use that experience to help you become even more fearless and confident.

- If you don't have the wardrobe to look the way you want or need to, you should be so full of confidence, talent and super-human charisma that when you walk into an audition, meeting, whatever, people are blinded by your presence. This does not mean you should be arrogant or unfriendly.

- Read everything, talk to everyone, learn, learn, learn. Whenever there is an opportunity to learn take it. Not just things related to your work. The more you know, the more information you have to draw from and the better you'll be at what you do.

- Be a student of people. No matter what genre you work in, you must understand human beings so you can make a human connection with your work.
- Don't limit your study of people to the United States. Pay attention to cultural nuances to deepen your understanding and sensitivity.
- Be professional! Meet deadlines, show up to work on time if not early. Know your lines, your blocking, your choreography, etc.
- Respect the people you work with. Diva behavior is funny to watch in a movie but no one wants to work with difficult people.
- Don't allow yourself to get star struck. That makes you a <u>fan</u> not a <u>professional</u>. For example, I worked as an extra on The Manchurian Candidate. In a scene with Denzel Washington, some of the extras were so star struck they broke through the barrier, forgot why they were there and swarmed Denzel for autographs. Many were sent home that day.
- Become wiser. Be impressed by actions instead of words.
- Finally, unless you decide to make a career change, ride out the storms. No matter how bleak it looks the storms always pass.
- Okay, one more thing, when people break your heart, don't let it destroy you. I'm not talking about intimate relationships. There will be people who will make promises of all sorts. "I'll give you a part

in the movie, I'll invest in your project, I need you to do the make-up for my show, you're the director I've been looking for", etc. I often wonder if people understand that your heart is in your work and when you are built up, then crushed by their lies, it's heart breaking. Keep going, you really will get over it. Just make a mental note that you will never do that to anyone.

Interview With Leslie Ford

I mentioned Leslie Ford, the Jazz musician and Founder of the Jazz Institute of New Jersey in two previous chapters. His story is so interesting that I thought it important to share. The following is the information he shared and is written in his voice:

It's a set back when an artist is blocked from doing his/her work. I did everything I could to support my family and myself. I also fought for time to still practice and perform. I took a correspondence course and learned how to be a locksmith. Even though I hated it, I worked hard to become good because I knew this was a skill that could provide a strong income stream.

I used to tell people that being a locksmith was my hobby. Music is my profession. This attitude made people respect me as a musician. My music really did help support my family. The locksmith work added to the financial pot.

When my second child was born, I came home one day and my wife said the baby had no milk. I was devastated. This drove me to put more energy into getting a day gig. A friend told me that Rutgers University was looking for a locksmith so I applied for the job and got it. During this time I was working full-time and very busy musically. I felt the need to concentrate on my spirituality to keep me balanced and keep my family together.

In this frame of mind and with the information I was absorbing by reading about the music business, I realized I needed to form my own company. This was a way to gain control of my time and my destiny. It is so important for artists to keep their creative juices flowing. If you don't you will feel hollow and you will eventually develop negative behaviors.

My goal was to stop trying to get a label to sign me. Instead, I would use my company as a means to record my music. I was relentless when it came to research. I needed to understand all aspects of the business. I was in the library so often reading a book called, *This Business of Music* that the librarian gave me an old copy when they received the new edition.

After gaining a solid understanding of the business side of music I formed my company, Leslie Ford & Group, LLC. I partnered with musician Radam Schawrtz to record my first CD. We both contributed original music and played on each other's compositions. We didn't have solid distribution but the CD proved to be a great promotional tool. I gave away so many copies that before long I had non-stop gigs. It also helped make another dream of mine possible.

Jazz saved my life. As a young person I was not interested in school, didn't see the point of it. When I did go I wasn't paying attention so at the age of sixteen I could not read. I was definitely headed for trouble.

One day my father introduced me to the trumpet and the music of Freddie Hubbard, a well-known Jazz musician. By listening to Mr. Hubbard's records, I was intrigued and suddenly wanted to know more about the music. I taught myself how to play the trumpet and eventually discovered a new vocabulary and a type of "controlling agent" that redirected my energy to a more positive direction.

My parents encouraged my new discovery but their economic conditions made it impossible for them to provide music lessons. Remembering these experiences led me to establish the Jazz Institute of New Jersey. I remained grateful for the life-altering impact Jazz music had on me as a teenager and vowed to give back to the community.

I brought together young talented musicians who shared my vision of passing on knowledge of the music. I wanted musicians who shared my desire to contribute to the social development of underprivileged youths. After years of careful planning and struggling to make this dream a reality, I succeeded in organizing a volunteer group of professional musicians to help develop an in-depth music history workshop entitled "Jazz History."

The workshop involved hands-on activity that introduced students and parents to various instruments and their origins, sounds and music concepts. But mainly, the workshop related life, discipline and education to the rudiments of music. The presentation drew enough positive reaction from students and parents that my dream to develop a comprehensive after-school program came to fruition. In our twenty-years of operation we have taught over nine hundred young people how to play instruments and deal with life.

My reputation was growing rapidly. Between the Jazz Institute and the constant work as a musician, my life was becoming financially lucrative. I held onto the locksmith job at Rutgers and involved the university in the Institute to a small extent. This made my time at the University bearable because it was now within the circle of my art.

By the way, once I began to read music fluently I realized I needed to learn to read words so by twenty, I was reading. I am an avid reader. Life is about overcoming obstacles and staying true to yourself. Artists have to find imaginative ways to fulfill their creative desires. Expressing our art is important to us.

Your art is your gift and you must cultivate this gift and share it. If you allow problems and money to stop this process, you will regret it the rest of your life. When things look dark and you momentarily don't see a way out, read. Read books that can help you stay focused on your goals. Study what successful people have gone through. Read books that will help you understand how this world works. Develop and strengthen your spirituality. Reading will give you survival ideas.

To musicians, I say learn to read music and play fluently! Learn every aspect of your instrument and practice, practice, practice! If you read music well and develop a great sound, you will be able to play in any environment. You can get work playing for commercials, recording artists, live shows, classical work...anything involving music. If you don't read music your chances to earn a living are limited.

The last thing I'll say is to never give up. Learn more, get better, put your children first if you have any, and develop skills that can make money. Don't forget to have fun along the way!

Interview with Al Santana, Cinematographer

Al Santana is an award winning independent filmmaker, educator, cinematographer and editor. In 2008 the Brooklyn Academy of Music (BAM) hosted a retrospective of Mr. Santana's films. He taught documentary film production and cinematography at CUNY (City University of New York) for over a decade. Below is a paraphrased description of his journey as a filmmaker/entrepreneur:

My introduction to filmmaking as a profession was through the industry. I viewed the progression thusly: you study your craft, you produce something tangible that will serve as your calling card (a reel), you seek out a job getting paid to do what you hopefully love to do. As a student I worked mainly on my independent projects-didn't do any work for hire. It was a very creative period, which involved a lot of exploration and experimentation.

When I became a professional cinematographer, the nature of the work dictated a different kind of discipline. I was no longer solely responsible to myself, but to many others who have invested, in many instances, large sums of money, and expected a "professional" result. I also found that often I was expected to conform creatively to a certain work style that was dictated by the format of a particular show. Experiencing this made it all the more important to continue my independent work in order to develop as an artist. For me it is not an all or nothing proposition. I believe one must be able to strike a balance between their commercial work and their personal work. However, I also believe the best possible scenario is when people are willing to pay for your personal independent vision.

My first job was with a public television station in New Jersey as a cinematographer. Later on I worked on several jobs in New York and joined the motion picture photographers union. This allowed me to work on TV productions, features and commercials.

At that time I also had an insatiable lust for travel. In fact much of my work was in Africa, South America and the Caribbean. While part of a producing team for a project that took me to Africa and Haiti, I contracted malaria and almost died. When I returned to the states, still recovering, a friend asked if I knew of anyone who would be interested in putting together a video division for the MTA (the transit authority in NYC).

Feeling like I needed to slow down and recuperate, along with my son having recently been born, I asked the friend if I could take the job. I was hired and for six years I ran the video and photography division of the New York City Transit Authority. This was a double-edged sword of sorts. On the one hand it provided financial stability and an opportunity to do some creative work, but on the other, it zapped all of my time and I was no longer able to pursue my independent work.

Finally, after six years I decided to leave that job. The up side of this is that I continued to work in my field. Upon leaving the NYCTA, I immediately began free-lancing; producing corporate videos and educational films. During this time, technological changes in the industry also meant I had to re-tool my skill-set in order to be competitive. I needed to have access to the training and the tools. I made a point to study everything. New and more powerful computers were emerging. New software that allowed one to have a production studio in their home was being developed. This was exciting and I knew I had to be a part of it.

The problem was figuring out how to afford to own the tools. I found myself being a burden on friends and acquaintances who, from time-to-time, were kind enough to let me use their equipment. But, it was not always available when I needed it. So, the first chance I got I jumped right in and taught myself how to assemble and operate a non-linear editing workstation. I also purchased digital cameras, a computer and editing software.

My interests also broadened from working primarily on documentaries to include narrative filmmaking. This also required a certain amount of study. I enrolled in screenwriting workshops, even took acting classes so that I could become familiar with the actor's process. I also taught classes and free-lanced as a videographer to keep a steady cash flow.

Eventually my apartment was becoming smaller, with all the equipment and a growing family. My wife and I always had a vision of owning our workspace. It is very important for an artist to have control of his/her space. Mental, physical and emotional space is needed to create. I have known many artists who have been evicted, had their belongings put out on the street and have lost all of their art. We were very fortunate because our long-held vision became a reality when we were able to purchase a house.

My advice to other artists is to find a balance between producing their art and being able to survive while doing it.

Understandably, It is real hard to think about creating when your lights are shut off or your stomach is growling. Find a way to finance the necessities and still work at your art. If you are not making a living at your art, try to integrate what you do, feel, and experience into your art and whatever work you do. For example, if you're a visual artist and you work at a bakery, use your artistic sensibilities to make the best looking bakery products imaginable or find another gig.

After all, our work reflects what is going on around us. It's not about getting wealthy so we can run away and forget the less fortunate in our community. If that's our reality we should see it in our work.

One way to keep working in your field is to learn the technical aspects of your industry. You can work as a technician to support yourself and still find time to do your projects. This has sustained me during my entire career. Even when I chose to work for the MTA, it was in a job that kept me connected to my field. You may work in several areas of your industry but it all adds up to experience. It makes you more proficient at what you do.

In this day and age, we are all students. It is important that one constantly studies, and adapt to new ways of working. Granted, there is the occasional fluke where a person is "discovered" or gets a "lucky" break but if the talent, discipline, and drive are absent that person will not survive the industry.

Finally, while working always search for opportunities to expand your reach to increase your income sources. This way you will never have to take a job outside your field again. Spike Lee is a good example of this entrepreneurial way of thinking. He makes his movies, developed a clothing line, started an advertising agency, wrote books, is working on a stage play, etc. Never stop searching for opportunities to earn a living within your art.

Take Care of You!

There is inherent physical and mental stress in the life of an artist. I don't need to back this statement up with research or medical findings. If you are a professional artist you can attest to this. If you are just embarking on this path, it won't take long to discover the truth in this statement. When actor Jim Carey was a child his whole family lived in their van for a while. Comedian Steve Harvey said that early in his career he lived in his car for a year. Writer/Director/Actor Tyler Perry also lived in his car while he toured his plays.

Does that sound like physical and mental stress? I was at a conference focused on getting movie scripts from the page to the screen and listened as Paul Schrader, the writer of the classic movie Taxi Drive, starring Robert Deniro, say that after a divorce he lived in his car for many months. When he became ill and went to the hospital he realized he had not spoken to another human being for months because he was ashamed of living in his car.

All the aforementioned men went on to great success but how does one survive and excel in spite of extreme diversity? Living in a car is certainly extreme but it's not the only problem that can destroy your mental and physical health if allowed. What about the constant stress of wondering where rent money is coming from each month? Facing eviction? Not knowing how you'll pay for food, heat and other necessities? Dealing with rejection in your career.

People whose only goal is to become famous and make tons of money don't usually stand up under this pressure.

Only those whose passion will not allow them to quit will fight their way through overwhelming adversity. You first have to understand that you are not the only one who has gone through extremely hard times.

It goes with the territory. I remember thinking when I started out as a playwright that if there are dues to pay, bring them on so I could get them out the way. Well, I found out it does not work that way. You can't control how or when it comes. Often things happen because we don't know any better. That is why earlier I encouraged you to create a plan for yourself that includes a way to make residual income.

No plan is guaranteed to develop the way it's laid out but at least it gives you direction. As adversity presents itself you will remember where you're headed and make adjustments. If you have no plan you get blindsided and just stand there trying to figure out what to do.

No matter what happens you will survive and grow if you;

- Have faith in God. However you view God you need a strong connection to give you faith and strength.
- Make every so-called failure a learning experience. Don't accept the concept of failure. You are not a failure.
- Don't pretend that you are not hurt. It hurts when you get disappointed and you have a lot at stake. Admit it hurts, think about it, and let it go.
- Are able to talk to someone who understands what you're working toward. If you have not found a few friends who understand, keep looking. An elderly

lady in a bank once gave me some words of encouragement that I needed at the time.

- Learn to work smarter. If your approach is not working, find new ways. Don't keep banging your head on the same door. Find a new door or at least a new angle from which to bang your head.

- Don't be afraid of hard work. Building your career is not a 9-5 job. If you want to be great at what you do, put in the time.

- If people close to you loose faith in your dream, don't let it kill what's inside of you. Once you succeed everyone around you will learn that perseverance, faith and hard work pays off.

- Really understand what it means to love and accept yourself.

- Realize you are not perfect and try to be the best person you can. You are a work in progress as we all are. Someone once told me not to see myself the way other people see me. To see myself as God sees us all, works in progress.

- Don't be afraid to ask for help. This can be very difficult depending who you are but sometimes you do need friends or family. Also, don't be crushed if your extended hand gets slapped. It happens.

- Read about what others have gone through. Henry Ford's family was about to commit him to an insane asylum because he kept talking about a horseless buggy and his experiments were not working. His car engine fired up and began running just in time to prevent his commitment.

- Keep getting better at what you do.
- Take an honest look at your skills and talent. Are you trying to be a dancer and can't pick up your leg? A writer who can't read? My point is get training for your art. You need to become the best you can be. In reality you're only competing against yourself.

Take care of yourself physically! I'm not talking about body types or "perfect" bodies. I'm talking about staying healthy! Eat whole foods. When money is scarce its easy to reach for the filling foods that aren't good for you. That's why I suggested putting together a survival box. Of course eventually that food will run out too but make choices that will keep you healthy.

You may have to scrape coins and bypass the foods you really want in favor of sustenance (i.e. beans, bananas, rice, chicken wings instead of the breast, etc.) but remember it won't last forever. I have been in supermarkets salivating over the beautiful fresh fruit and vegetables but could only afford a bag of apples, beans, rice, peanut butter and jelly and the cheap, store brand whole wheat bread.

It's very frustrating to stand in the midst of plenty and not to be able to afford what you want and need. You can stay healthy and satisfied if you make it an adventure. Become the master of the "one pot" meal. Pick up marked down foods and experiment mixing items you like. A friend of mine is writing a book about beans because she's had to eat so many of them.

There's another side to the whole starving artist thing. I gained weight instead of wasting away. I lived on marked down breads and pasta as well as vegetables and fruit, mostly bananas because they got marked down often. When I finally did get more money I would eat things I had not been able to afford. It's funny how you crave all kinds of food during lean times. Often, what made me decide whether or not to attend an event was if they had refreshments. That would be my dinner or lunch.

During business meetings, if others were buying, I would order dishes that had large servings then eat a small portion so I could take the rest home for later. This is why when we ran the NJ Movie Maker's Network, I would always have food at our events. I knew there were artists who needed to eat. I was not wrong because there were rarely many leftovers after the events.

Take vitamins and pay attention to exercise. Exercise is a great way to keep stress in check. If you can't afford a gym and where you live is too dangerous to walk, just turn on some music and dance in your house. No matter what your art form is, all of the arts are physically demanding. So make sure you get exercise.

A filmmaker I know finally got financing to shoot his movie. There was a scene where the principal actor had to run up a flight of stairs. It took them half a day to shoot the scene because the actor could not make it up the stairs without almost passing out. They had to shoot him running in short takes and piece it all together during editing.

Why work so hard to get a break and when it comes you're not able to rise to the occasion. That filmmaker will never use that actor again and by him telling his story, others will stay away from that actor too. I reiterate, keep working to stay on top of your game! No matter what your size or body type keep your focus on being healthy.

Finally, while you are working to reach your goals and absorbed with your craft, take time to enjoy your life. This can be something as simple as enjoying a breeze, appreciating a beautiful flower, and living in the smile of a child. Don't put off living. Enjoy the journey as you work hard. Enjoy that special someone in your life because it can be hard for people to be in a relationship with an artist.

I remember hearing my mother fuss at my father because on the way home with his pay for the week he stopped at the music store to buy manuscript paper and reeds for his horn. She wanted to buy enough food to last two weeks and he "blew" money on his music. If there is someone in your life who loves and understands you, enjoy that and treat him or her well. After I got divorced I stayed single for a long time. I used to joke and say what man would put up with me using rent money to make a movie?

You are the center of your work. If you are not healthy, how will you ever be successful? Very creative people see the world differently. We're usually very sensitive. Your work requires that you open yourself up to a plethora of feelings and emotions. This leaves you vulnerable in many ways. If you are beginning to feel depressed and can't shake it, if fear and/or insecurity try to take you over, if you have serious trouble sleeping, get some help.

It's really important to ask for help when you feel parts of your life are out of control. Often minor adjustments will help you put things in perspective and diminish the problem. Not getting help turns small issues into large ones. No matter what, do not self medicate. This will only make matters worse, kill your skill and cut your life short. I have mentioned this previously because we have lost far too many gifted artists to substance abuse.

Remember to see yourself as an entrepreneur, a work in progress, and don't let mistakes hold you back. Learn from them and keep going.

Interview with Torrie Sloan

Mr. Sloan is an entrepreneur with over ten years of experience and success as a professional network marketer. He also has put in several years in the banking industry in the areas of personal and business banking as well as management. The following is his advice for artists/entrepreneurs:

I have learned from my experience and watching others that the biggest barrier to a person's success is usually him/herself. So the first thing I tell anyone is to read books that focus on personal development and self-help. This will change your perception and prevent you from sabotaging yourself by constantly thinking about how hard things will be for you. If you focus on the fear of the unknown instead of moving forward you will not get a positive result. People who are successful have a different way of thinking.

The successful person evaluates what needs to be done, asks how it can be done and proceeds to find the answers. This person realizes that obstacles are challenges not the end of the road. The person with a defeatist mentality says, "I can't do it, its too hard." If you believe there are answers to a situation you will eventually find them. This attitude presents you with options. Below are a few suggestions;

1. Keep a log or daily planner and write down everything you do each hour or each day. Then analyze how you spend your time. This helps with time management. Be honest with yourself and eliminate time wasting activities.

2. Consider a part-time or night job as an income stream. What you do depends on your circumstances but don't be afraid of working hard to get what you need. People on the outside don't see all the sacrifice that goes into success. When they see a person "blow up" in their minds its "luck." Don't be afraid to push yourself and make sacrifices.

3. Take a serious look at network marketing as an income stream. Its no longer taboo. In the present challenging economic climate you cannot depend on a job alone. Unlike a job, in network marketing you cannot be fired. Your business and income is developed based on the time you put in.

4. Be sure you choose network-marketing opportunities that are legitimate.
If a company interests you contact your local Better Business Bureau and/or the Direct Selling Association. If these two sources are not aware of the company, and/or the company does not have a good report with these entities, leave them alone. It may sound good on the Internet but your research must extend beyond what the company says about itself.

5. Pick something that you can be passionate about so you can enjoy the venture and not feel burdened.

6. Remember everything you do is based on building positive relationships. If

you get involved with a company just to make money and have no passion you will not succeed because people will not trust you. You never know how the relationships you build in different areas of your life will serve your artistic needs as you move forward.

7. Learn the value of teamwork in everything you do. Whether you get involved with network marketing or not, a team of like-minded people is stronger than a person standing alone. Network marketing is based on teamwork. How can you apply this approach to your art?

Lastly, artists and everyone should learn how to deal with banks. Be discriminating when it comes to choosing a bank. Don't be sucked in by the ones with the best commercials and advertising. Not all banks are for you.

1. Huge national banks have too many fees (both obvious and hidden) and they generally are not consumer friendly unless you maintain a hefty deposit in your account. I don't mean a few hundred or even a few thousand dollars. The home office will probably be in another state. This means no one in the branch can make decisions without contacting someone in another state.

2. Community Banks are a better choice. The fees are usually less than national banks. The people in the bank will get to know you (if you work on building relationships) and it's easier to get

immediate answers. In most cases, decisions can be made by the branch manager, head teller or your business banker.

3.   Credit unions are one of the best-kept secrets in the industry. They offer the same services as banks but generally have lower interest rates, fewer fees and their services will be more personal.

*<u>Note</u>: Mr. Sloan is available for one-on-one consultations, speaking engagements or conference calls. He can be contacted via email: <u>mrtorriesloan@inbox.com</u>

The Cumulative Effect

Not everyone is successful at the same time. I saw Whoopi Goldberg being interviewed for a show in New York. One of the things she talked about was how her circle of friends reacted once she became "successful." She wondered why they were upset instead of being happy for her since she would have been excited for them. She eventually realized that they were hurt. Why did it happen for her and not for them? This reaction surprised Ms. Goldberg.

Its important for all of us to realize that not everyone reaches his or her goals at the same time. You should be exuberant when someone you know "makes it" because that means you can too. Positive energy will push you forward while a spirit of jealously will hold you back.

It can take years to reach the level of success you need. However, don't overlook the steps of success you have gained along the way. Every time you accomplish something, it's another success step, inching you closer to where you want to be. You also learn a lot along the way. People may look at you and say, "You've been at this twelve years why haven't you succeeded?" More than likely, you will ask this of yourself.

Even if no one else realizes this, you must understand that success is a process. It's a culmination of everything you do over a period of time. Sure, some people seem to get big breaks quickly while others go through the process. Whether you're a real overnight success or someone whose been working for years, we all pay our dues one way or another. Look at the singer Brittany Spears.

She hit it big in her late teens, early twenties. Then she had a personal set back that became public. The woman could not grieve in private. Her personal problems were broadcast daily for several months. How damaging is that? Can you imagine having a very private, hurtful situation constantly in the public eye? People followed her every move, taking pictures and intruding. Eventually she got help and hopefully things evened out for her.

With all of this behind her I'm sure Ms. Spears is a wiser person. However, the point is, while it may seem she had it easy and paid few dues to achieve a solid career, she paid dues on another level. I repeat, you never know when or how but you will pay. Its part of the learning curve. By the way, Brittany did pay some dues along the way as a child performer.

If you begin to feel like you're wasting your time and doubt yourself, evaluate your accomplishments. How much have you learned along the way? We work so hard to move forward that we forget to take stock of what has been achieved. During my low money, slow accomplishment times, I would Google my name and read all the entries just to remind myself that I am not standing still no matter how it seemed.

Even if your name is not in the search engines yet, just make a list of everything you've done and all you're working on. More than likely you will be encouraged. How can you take the experience you've gained and use it to make money? How can you use it to change your conversation? What do I mean by this?

If you really look at your experiences, you can approach people differently. Instead of saying, "I'm working to break into the business", "I'm trying to raise money for…" you can now say, "I have experience!" "Experience has taught me…." Realizing that you have actually had successes, changes your attitude about yourself. Take stock in what you've done. Even if your only experience is in college or some type of professional training, use it! The thing is to be in the business.

You have to be a walking advertisement for yourself. If money is low, keep one power outfit that you wear when necessary. This is what you wear to meet money people or to auditions that call for that look. If you have to meet these folks a second time just add a new touch to the outfit. A different tie or shirt, an accessory, whatever it takes. No matter what you wear physically, you should exude success and confidence.

I was at a press conference for a well-known theater company early in my career. There were many celebrities there and a host of "wanna be's." One lady who was working the room, looking for "important people" started a conversation with me and when I said I was a playwright she responded, "Do you want to be a playwright or are you already a playwright?" She waited for an answer. I said, "I am a playwright!"

In my thinking this was a stupid question. You either are or you aren't. If I'm writing plays I'm a playwright. If I'm dancing and training, I'm a dancer. If I'm playing my instrument and performing, I'm a musician. What this woman really wanted to know was if I was accomplished and well known. That's a different question. Needless to say I politely moved away from her. Define yourself and keep working!

Be firm with yourself. Even if you are not famous and don't have a dollar in your pockets, that does not mean you are not in the business. You're in it, just working to get paid. If you see yourself as trying instead of being and doing, you will never progress. I really loved it when the musician Leslie Ford said he would tell people being a locksmith was his hobby and music his profession. That is the attitude that moves you forward.

Actor Harrison Ford was working as a carpenter when he got the role of Han Solo in "Star Wars". What if his attitude was, I'm a carpenter who is trying to make it as an actor? Do you think he would have been able to convince the people making the decisions that he was Han Solo? No because he would have lacked the power to bring the role to life.

Personal power, charisma, the ability to make people believe who you are, all come from confidence, belief in yourself and talent. Confidence comes from passion and being prepared. Stand on your past accomplishments no matter how small they seem and continue to grow in your field. The bottom line is if you don't believe in yourself why should anyone else believe in you?

I don't care if your mother, father, wife, husband, children friends...the closest people don't not have faith in your passion and abilities, you have to. If you don't maybe this is more of a hobby for you and that's fine. If that's the case, find a career that fits you better. You may want to stay in the business but in a different capacity. How many agents used to be performers? Never give up on yourself. There is always a way to fill your artistic needs. Just keep your eyes open.

Financing Your Projects

No matter what type of artist you are, you need some amount of money to constantly produce new work and/or promote projects that have been completed. The stories about maxing out credit cards or borrowing from friends and family might be good for one time. However, if you want to build a career your skills for capitalizing your projects have to constantly grow.

It can be very frustrating when your projects are under capitalized. You never have enough money to do all that needs to be done. Consequently, either the quality suffers or you don't have the funds to effective promote your work. Maybe the quality is great, but the project is not completed. What can be done?

To begin with, if the money is low, find a way to produce a very small representation of your work. We all have a vision so see if you can reduce it to something small enough that it is affordable but shows off what you do in a high quality format. For instance, if a musician / singer / songwriter wants to cut a disc and shoot a music video but has little money, why not just record the hook of your tune and shoot a 30 second video around the hook. It will look more like a movie trailer and at the same time drive that hook into the viewer's memory.

This approach also makes it easier to present because it's so short. As a make up artist, perhaps you don't have the cash for a state-of-the-art video or hard copy portfolio. Can you work with a good camera operator and a few models (who also need a reel) and shoot samples of your work put to music? You don't need runway models. Use people who have the look you're trying to sell. Again, keep it to 30 seconds.

The point is, you must be extremely creative. Don't lament about not having the money and wait until it comes before you get started. Unless you can show what you do, it will be extremely difficult to attract the money you need. We all take risks but make sure your risks are calculated. Don't jump out there and try to produce a full-blown project when you know in advance you have no where near the money you need. This will end in hardship and incredible frustration. It can also ruin your professional reputation with your team members. Above all be honest about your situation so the people who work with you will not feel like they have been used.

Once you have your 30 second sample, you can proceed to show off your work. Another alternative is to produce your project in steps. If a filmmaker has a budget of $500,000.00 and only raises $50,000.00, can he/she produce the first ten minutes of the movie and call it a short? Perhaps in the film festival circuit it can pick up some interest for the filmmaker and lead to more money. Even if it wins no awards, it can now be said that it was in several festivals and well received.

That being said, how do you attract investors for your projects?

1. No matter what type of work you do, you absolutely must write a business plan of some kind. You need to come up with 5-10 Cohesive pages that explain;
   a) What your project is about.
   b) Who is the audience.

c) How you will reach them?
d) How will the project make money?
e) How much money it will make?
f) How long it will take to make this money?
g) How much do you need to produce the work?
h) How you will pay it back to investors?
i) How long it will take to pay it back?
j) How much profit will they make once the investment is repaid?
k) What will be their percentage of the profits?
l) What is your track record?
m) Who are the members of your team?
n) What are their track records?
o) How long will they be able to participate in profit making?
p) Who else is doing something similar to your project?
q) How is your project different?
r) What will make you stand out in the market?
s) How have others with similar projects fared?
t) How much money did they make?

The bottom line is how much do you need and how much will the investor make? Remember that you are an entrepreneur. You are not asking someone to do you a favor. You are presenting them with an opportunity to make money from your work. You have the talent and they have the money. You can research what business plans should look like. Once you understand the basic format, you can cater the information to fit your genre.

Remember to keep it short and to the point (5-10 pages). If the potential investor wants more information, put it together and give them what they want. You also must try to understand the investor's perspective. How hard is it to get money out of your pocket? People who invest money do it because they want to turn a profit. You have to get them excited about what you're doing but excitement without the potential to make a profit will not go far. The person may also ask how much you have put into the project.

Anticipating this question keep records of the amount of money you've spent trying to bring the project to life. This includes transportation costs, office supplies, copying, research, writing, meetings, etc. Establish an hourly rate for your time, calculate the amount of hours spent and include that amount. Another thing most artists don't consider is sweat equity. This is all the time and years you've spent developing your talent and learning. If the person you approach does not understand this, turn it around and ask them what the amount of time and energy they put into their education and experience is worth. Your skills are no less than theirs, just different. Again, be friendly and polite, not confrontational. You want the money.

Most artists including me, don't want to be bothered with this end of the business. If you have several thousand dollars to pay someone to write a business plan for you that's fine. Otherwise, suck it up and do it yourself. The process actually helps you think through your project. You'll be surprised how much you learn about what you're planning to embark upon!

Beware of Venture Capitalists and Banks. Venture Capitalists are sharks who don't care about anything but money. More than likely they will want more than 50% of your project. In order to own your work or company, you must maintain 51% ownership. Anything less than that makes you the investor's employee. If one person wants 50% or more than one person invests they will split up the 50% you allowed for investors.

For example, if you need $1M and you find four people willing to put up $250,000.00 each, then each investor will own 12.5% of the project equaling a total of 50%. Another important thing to remember is to make it clear that the investors only own part of the project they invest in. They do not own part of your company or any other projects you have done previously or in the future. Why is this important? If that is not clear and you do other projects, it will be harder to raise money because you'll have people from the old project laying claim to everything you do.

Consider Ancillary rights when developing your plan. Ancillary rights are linked to any side products that develop from your project. For instance from a movie a book may be developed, posters, toys, clothing, etc. Just look at "Star Wars" and how many products were sold with Star Wars themes. These are other income streams and investors must be allowed to participate in them.

The more opportunities you can show for money to be made, the stronger your presentation. Along with the business plan you should include an agreement that can be signed to close the deal. If the person does not sign on right away and needs time to think, you should be able to leave an agreement then follow–up to close. The worse thing you can do is get the person(s) excited then say, "I'll get back to you as soon as I draw up the agreement." You have to get them on board while the interest is there. This also shows that you are professional and thorough.

Write up an agreement that includes everything you can think of then take it to an attorney. This will save you money. The attorney will consider what you have then put it in a legal format. Once you have an agreement drawn up by an attorney, you can use it over and over as long as the project is similar. All you will have to do is change the names, numbers, etc. Understand that the investor may want to make some changes. This is common. Just have the attorney examine the changes before you sign.

Regarding banks, understand that any loan originating from a bank must start to be repaid 30 to 90 days after you get the money. If you are able to get a bank loan, even if you disguise it as a personal loan, it has to be paid back according to their schedule. Will your project be profitable in 30 to 90 days? In most cases the answer is no. It can take six months to two years before any entertainment project becomes profitable so how will you make the loan payments? Will you use your personal resources? Bad idea, you may wind up living in the street.

Some take out more money than needed for the project so they can have a cushion for repayments. This may work but you have to really plan and be careful not to get in over your head. If you can't go to banks and Venture Capitalists, where do you find money?

There is no hard and fast rule or guarantee but here are some suggestions:

1. Consider friends and family members but don't let them use their total savings just in case the project does not make money.
2. Look at the people you do business with. Your contractor, accountant, the owner of the store you patronize regularly, beautician, barber, business acquaintances, your doctor, dentist, etc.

Who you approach is only limited by your creativity. Be able to explain your offering in 30 seconds saying what you want to do, what it will cost and how much the investor will make. If there is more interest move to your second presentation which should take no longer than 10 minutes. The next step is to sit down and go over the business plan which can take as long as the person has questions.

Dress according to whom you approach. If you're meeting with a successful artist you may not have to do the suit and tie thing or power suit for women but if you're meeting with an accountant, doctor…someone more formal, dress the part. An extremely successful producer once told me he wears whatever will work for the person he approaches for money. This is because you want to enter the person's world and help them feel comfortable with you. You can always add things to make you unique and show your personality but the goal is to fit into their world.

You are legally required to include in the agreement that there is a chance the person may not be able to recoup his/her investment. The attorney will know how to word it. This is why its important to work with an entertainment attorney. He/she will know the language and the business.

There are so many ways to raise money, It all depends on how much you need and how far your imagination will roam. Remember that we now live in a global community. There may be money and partnerships available from other countries. Do research and find out where the money may be available. This is another reason you should attend conferences and expos. If accountants are having a conference in your area shouldn't you be there?

For one thing attending the conference will help you understand their language and their concerns. During lunch or in forums you can approach people and tell them what you do and what you need. Learn how to listen. People on panels or in the workshops may say something that lets you know this is a person you need to speak with.

Be open to new ideas. Think about what types of people and professions deal with money. Go to their websites, read Forbes (the capitalist tool) and other magazines that deal with money. The library has the Wall Street Journal, why aren't you there reading it? This is how you get ideas about getting the money you need.

A few years ago, a man in a small town in New Jersey put jars in local stores asking to contribute to a local filmmaker's new movie. He left the jars in the stores for a month and made enough to shoot his small movie. Of course this could only work in a very small town but it worked. I read in a book about the human brain that we are capable of learning 24 million new bits of information everyday. Allow your mind to run wild.

Be honest, include investors in the credits, printed materials, internet announcements, basically, offer them visible recognition for their efforts. If you are not a good speaker and totally uncomfortable approaching people, find someone close to you who can be your spokesperson. In return, offer this person a small percentage of the project. You may also have to pay for their transportation and meeting expenses. Remember, obstacles are only opportunities to learn more and be creative. Watch out for unscrupulous people who will waste your time with promises. And don't fear rejection. Eat that stuff and keep going!

Plan For Your Success!

It was stated earlier that you need to make plans to keep income streaming into your life while climbing the mountain to artistic success. Once that is working, you have to plan to be successful. Once you reach the serious income-producing plateau in your field, you can go from being broke to having money in a very short period of time. Here are a few things you should have in place to be ready:

- An Entertainment Attorney. If you cannot afford to retain one yet, start gathering cards and have conversations with several and decide who you will work with. You need to know this before the contracts start rolling in so you can respond immediately when you do begin to receive them.
- An accountant who is familiar with tax laws related to entertainment. Not all accountants are familiar with entertainment tax laws. An accountant can save you money and keep you out of trouble with the IRS even before you make your millions.
- A Public Relations/Publicity person. Again, you may not be able to keep a person on retainer yet but you can get advice and pay for little things along the way until the big hit. You need the right people to know what you are doing to create a buzz about you. This helps brand you and increase your worth.
- A business bank account. Remember what was said about banks. Choose a small bank or credit union and forge relationships with the staff. This will make it easier to do business with them. Do your

best to keep your business money and personal money separate. This may be hard when you don't have much but do it.

- Have in mind an administrative assistant you can hire. You will no longer be able to do everything yourself. You will need help. This person will not be your slave but someone who can help with the paperwork, schedules, appointments, etc. Someone who can think on their feet.

- A stylist and make-up consultant (even if you are a male). As you become more visible you want to be sure your look does not work against you. There's the way you look knocking around the house and the way you present yourself in public. This does not mean you are required to wear all designer clothing and accessories. But you do need to know what colors work for you on TV, on stage, in photos and other helpful advice from a stylist. No matter what level of make-up you use, you do need a person to make sure you look good in all media. Men may not wear lipstick and eye make-up but shining can be an issue.

- Someone to take care of your hair. You've come this far why not look your best. Men also need this service.

- Someone to help you stay balanced. We all need someone to tell us the truth, have our best interest at heart and disagree when necessary. This can be a family member, good friend, professional associate, etc.

- A spiritual frame of reference to make sure you don't get lost.

This may seem silly if you're still struggling to pay rent. However, preparing for success also puts you in the frame of mind to be successful. This should be part of your career plan. Be ready!

Take Control of Your Career!

Once you have done the mental preparation, are working on developing income streams to support your day- to-day needs? Do you realize that you are an artist/entrepreneur? How can you take control of your career? If you have implemented the things mentioned previously in this book, you are well on your way.

Your conversation is more direct, confident and informed. You have a strong working knowledge of your industry and related industries. You are developing your brand, You. Now you have to own the equipment needed to give you the upper hand. You have to be able to make a presentation anywhere, anytime. What you need depends on your craft.

No matter what your artistic focus, everyone needs to own a computer (the type based on your needs) and printer. You also need a line for Internet access or a wifi card and a telephone. Before you do anything else, these items are the first investment in your career.

Filmmakers need to at least own a consumer camcorder if you cannot afford to purchase a professional video camera. The pro camera can always be rented. Having the ability to record ideas and things you find interesting is critical and will sharpen your skills. Dancers, singers, visual artists, make-up artists, musicians, designers, directors, basically all artists need to be able to take still or moving pictures of their ideas and creations.

These ideas and/or creations can be shown to potential investors, people who will be working with you or uploaded to Internet sites as needed. You also need portable media devices based on your field like iPods, MP3 players, portable CD players, digital voice recorders, flash drives and batteries. It is very important that you purchase these tools from a place with sales professionals who will give you honest advice based on your needs. You also need quality equipment that is affordable. Nothing is worse than setting up to show someone your work and the device does not work.

I suggest that you do not go to just an electronics store. That is fine for amateurs. You are a professional who needs professional equipment. One store that provides good consultations is B&H Photo-Video/Pro Audio. If you are in the New York City area the store is located at 420 Ninth Ave. They also have a comprehensive website allowing equipment to be purchased from anywhere in the country: www.bhphotovideo.com. If you are not sure and need to speak to a consultant call 212-239-7500. B& H has discount prices and great equipment.

Do not be afraid of equipment. No matter what your age, you must stay current to work. You cannot take a VHS tape to an agent or anyone else to show your work. Digital equipment will allow you to upload your still photos, sound recording, or moving images to a file that can be emailed or texted to the party of concern. Focus on making it easy and convenient for your work to be seen. Presentation is an important part of the success process.

If you are not yet able to purchase equipment be extremely creative. You can purchase disposable cameras. Your possibilities are endless if you let your imagination run free. Don't wait for people to "discover" you. Instead, present yourself.

Find a way to get your projects moving. If you don't have much money, think small. Do a small no/low budget project. Make it excellent and use it as leverage to keep growing. Torrie Sloan spoke of team building in his interview. This can really be important when you're in the early stages of branding your work. For example, if you are shooting a short movie, find other artists who need to brand their work. Talk to stylists, make- up artists, cinematographers, hair stylists, photographers, sound engineers, illustrators, lighting technicians, composers, etc. In other words, all the people you need to produce a highly professional project. If everyone works with a high level of professionalism you will all have an outstanding reel to ad to your professional arsenal.

There are many people who try to recruit artists for projects with no or low pay. Make sure that the people you sign on with are working at high levels of professionalism. Otherwise, the end product may not prove useful. However, if the project will increase the length of your resume it may be worth your while.

While taking control of your career remember its all about decisions. Every step you take involves making a decision. Who will you work with, what's your next step, who do you need to connect with, etc. Also remember there is a fine line between taking control and being an arrogant prick that will turn people off. Treat everyone with respect and you will be ahead of the game.

In Conclusion

We all begin our journey with a vision or idea of the career peaks we want to reach. The journey may have many winding paths both professionally and personally. Before you realize it years have passed. Are you a failure if you don't reach your original goal? We have to consider this question because others can never be as hard on us as we are on ourselves.

As you grow in your career you may find that your original idea grows in a different direction. If your passion is acting and along the way you discover that you love working with children and wind up running a children's theater are you a failure? How about the make-up artist who mastered theatrical make-up and wanted to develop creatures and all kinds of special effects for movies. If this person stumbles upon teaching people with horrible scars how to disguise them and makes it a career is he/she a failure?

If your passion leads you to a place that was not your original vision you are not a failure. It's all about the journey anyway. What you learn along the way will lead you to a destination that you may not have considered. What's important is that you are happy and can live a comfortable life. We must learn to have fun along the way and enjoy the journey as much as possible.

If you are an artist/entrepreneur, take control of your career, stay on top of your game, never stop learning, learn how to take rejection and keep moving forward without missing a beat. Work on multiple income streams, develop a spiritual base for your life, manage your time wisely, love yourself, treat others with respect, put your children first (if you have any) and never give in to fear (for more than a few minutes). These things lead to success! Some see artists as children who don't want to grow up. You know this is not true. You are a professional, an entrepreneur, and a mirror for humanity.

No matter what your art is, in some way, artists help people to see themselves, to dream, to grow, to learn new things, to feel, to imagine and hopefully to change. Just remember that you are responsible for what you produce. Your work can either be uplifting or destructive. The choice is yours but it is a choice.

Pay attention to the "behind the scenes" people. During the five years I ran the NJ Movie Maker's Network, whenever we had a "star" do a presentation the attendance was incredible. This was good for us because it made money. On the other hand, when we had "behind the scenes" industry people facilitate a workshop, attendance would be lighter. It surprised me when people did not understand that the actors and one news anchor speaking at our events could share information from their perspective but could not hire a person or green light a project.

It was important to listen to actors, which is why we invited them but that's only one piece of the puzzle. Too many artists were star struck. Shelly Palmer, who at the time was the Director of New Media for the National Academy of Television Arts and Sciences (NATAS the people who give the Emmy Awards) presented a phenomenal workshop on new media and explained how each one could be used to advance careers. Only fifteen people showed up. This was in 2004, on the cusp of the new media explosion.

I spoke to a friend in Manhattan who did similar programs for people in the music industry. He had the same experience. If they had "star" producers or entertainers headline a program it was packed. When they had "non-star" producers, A&R people, publicists, etc. on panels attendance would be light. He even had panels where the aforementioned professionals would listen to CD's and give advice. That was not the attraction, the "star' was the draw.

If you want to make great connections and get information that can really advance your career, go to events that feature behind the scenes people. If the person presenting is not known to you, so what? Pay attention to what they do. Big star studded events are fine and you can pick up some information but don't limit yourself to these functions. Listen to the ones who keep the wheels grinding behind the scenes. Depending on the event, most of "grinders" will speak with you (briefly) after the presentation.

Promote yourself and your work! If you don't who will? Until you can hire a publicist or PR person you have to do this. Learn how to use the new media to get the word out about what you do. There is a musician name Rob Murat whose music I like and can't wait to see him perform. I became aware of him on MySpace. I listened to his music and dropped a line saying it was good. Since then I receive constant updates & short videos (via email) about his career. He has to be the hardest working man on MySpace. I'm sure he has a team working to keep him so visible. Remember I talked about the importance of building a team earlier.

The point is to put in the work. Being an artist means not only do you have to work at developing your talent but you also have work hard to create opportunities to work. If you consider the things discussed in this book and put in the work, you will not be a starving artist in the 21st century. You will become an artist/entrepreneur who is in a position to make decisions about his/her career, works hard, becomes successful and hopefully will never miss a meal unless you're just too busy to eat. But don't even let that happen too often.

www.ingramcontent.com/pod-product-compliance
Lightning Source LLC
Chambersburg PA
CBHW071232170526
45165CB00003B/1074